How To Refocus Your Life

Life Lessons™ For Your Success

Volume 1

Procrastination
Self-Doubt
Lack of Focus

Dr. Herbert Harris
With
Greatest Victory Contributors

The LifeSkill® Institute, Inc.
P.O. Box 302
Wilmington, NC 28402

First Printing: November 2025

Published by:

LifeSkill Institute, Inc. SAN: 255-8440

P.O. Box 302

Wilmington, NC 28402

(800) 570-4009

Emai: herbert@herbertharris.com

Websites: www.herbertharris.com-
www.lifeskillinstitute.org

****

Library of Congress Cataloging-in-Publication Data

ISBN: 978-1-890199-13-5 paperback edition

ISBN; 978-1-890199-11-1 kindle edition

TABLE OF CONTENTS

FOREWORD

When Dr. Herbert Harris told me that he was writing a new book, I said, *"Sign me up. I'll write the foreword."*

I have known Herbert for over 35 years. We met through Ali Yasin while working with Dick Gregory in marketing the Bahamian Diet, Dick's nutritional and weight-loss product.

Herbert and I were both starting out on our speaking and training journeys. Herbert was focused on network marketing and personal development while I found my stride as a motivational speaker.

Over the years, I have watched Herbert become a master network marketing trainer and personal development and success expert. His writings, lectures, and training have impacted thousands of lives.

When Dr. Harris wrote his international bestseller, **The Twelve Universal Laws of Success**, I knew it would be an important personal development book for entrepreneurs and those seeking life transformation. This book has achieved international success, being translated into numerous languages including Chinese, French, Italian, Romanian, and Spanish.

Herbert's new book, **Life Lessons™ for Your Success**, is the next evolution and application of the principles included in **The Twelve Universal Laws of Success.**

In **Life Lessons™ for Your Success**, Herbert applies the principles in **The Twelve Universal Laws of Success** to specific life situations and challenges. His treatment of issues such as: Refocusing Your Life, How to Overcome Self-Doubt and Procrastination, shows a deep understanding and practical approach to handling these very common obstacles to success, achievement, and happiness.

Life Lessons™ for Your Success is an important series that covers and offers solutions to many of the challenges most of us will experience at different times throughout our lives.

A unique aspect of this book is – in addition to the instructive content provided by Dr. Harris

– it also includes commentaries by selected contributors who were interviewed in his **"Success Talk Podcast."**

These commentaries give insight into the lives, challenges, and victories of the selected contributors. I was impressed with the stories shared by the contributors who gave very personal testimonies of their struggles and powerful advice based on their experiences.

I highly recommend **Life Lessons™ for Your Success** as a powerful resource for handling life challenges that can undermine your success. This book is a step-by-step guide to help you refocus your life, overcome self-doubt, procrastination, and many other challenges that will surely arise on your success journey.

It will become the ***"Go-To"*** book in this time of transition, uncertainty, and opportunity.

Les Brown,

The Greatest Motivational Speaker in the World

Website: https://lesbrown.com/

ACKNOWLEDGMENTS

Sandra Spaulding Hughes, for her love, support, and encouragement that have been a blessing in every aspect of my life.

Carolyn J. Blue, whose friendship and support have been invaluable.

Burke Hedges, for his friendship and coaching that helped me grow and succeed as an entrepreneur, network marketer, and author.

Coach David L. Smile, whose encouragement and guidance helped me find my calling as a transformational speaker and personal development trainer.

Sade Thomson, whose creative assistance helped us manage and grow our branding and social media presence.

Ricky Young, whose commitment to personal development through his radio program *"What's In Your Hands"* has impacted the lives of thousands of listeners to more than 1,000 inspirational shows.

Dawn Lovell, whose assistance in editing and improving this book was invaluable.

GREATEST VICTORY CONTRIBUTORS

Dr. Rubye Braye

Iva Brito

Bryce Britton

Ken Brown

Princess Castleberry

Jay Clark

Karen Creecy

Oscar Joe Dais

Tonya Debnam

Hikia Dixon

Kyle Dixon

Stephanie Gore

Dr. James Graham

Cassandra Henderson

Junniej Jackson

Chris Johnson

Rev. Bernette Jones

Gary Jones

Carrie McIntyre

Steve Miller

Derek Phillips

Jason Roberts

Roland & Dorensa Roberts

Will Smith

Coach David Smile

Herman Taylor

Stan White

Troy Whitehurst

INTRODUCTION

Our book, Life Lessons™ **for Your Success,** is dedicated to all who purchased our book The ***Twelve Universal Laws of Success*** and used it to transform their lives.

I am forever grateful that you have allowed me to be a part of your life journey.

Description

Over the last twenty years, I have had the opportunity to interact with thousands of you who read our book, attended our classes, workshops, and seminars.

As a result, I found that certain issues, challenges, and obstacles impede our progress on our success journey.

Our goal in writing Life Lessons™ **for Your Success** is to identify these challenges and provide ways to address them.

Each chapter covers a particular life challenge that undermines your efforts on your success journey in life and in business.

These challenges are addressed in a concise, straightforward manner that provides insight, direction, and solutions.

The objective of each chapter is to provide understanding, context, and easy to follow steps for addressing and overcoming life's challenges.

Greatest Victory Contributors

While writing the Life Lessons™ **for Your Success**, I was conducting a series of interviews for our Success Talk Podcast.

As the Success Talk interviews were reviewed, it became obvious that many of the achievers being interviewed had also faced and overcome life challenges and obstacles on their success journeys.

There were times when no one believed in them. Sometimes they doubted themselves.

There were days when they felt like David facing Goliath – when everything was at stake.

When all was said and done, these contributors dug deep, ignored the doubters, and achieved their "Greatest Victory."

I decided that our readers need to know their stories.

The story of how these contributors achieved their "Greatest Victory" may be just the thing our readers need to be inspired and hang in there to resolve their own challenges.

GREATEST VICTORY CONTRIBUTORS IN VOLUME 1

Platinum Contributors

Jay Clark

Tonya Debnam

Rev. Bernette L. Jones

Diamond Contributors

Princess Castleberry

Cassandra Henderson

Troy Whitehurst

Success Honor Roll

Chris Johnson

Derek Phillips

Jason Roberts

MESSAGE TO OUR READERS

Today Is Yesterday's Tomorrow

Today is the actual result of the effectiveness of your plans. If you fully utilized each and every hour available yesterday, then you have done all you can to maximize your possibilities for achievement, reward, and success today.

If you wasted those precious moments of yesterday in frivolous, unproductive endeavors, your rewards would come in like fashion today.

Along with the results of your previous efforts, today also contains the seeds of tomorrow's possibilities.

Today embraces the opportunity to make tomorrow the way you want it to be.

Each day represents the results and proof of your previous endeavors, together with an opportunity for change in the future.

Seize upon this daily opportunity for change with a positive attitude and a definite plan.

Put this plan into immediate action through continuous, effective work.

The results of your efforts today will surely appear as tomorrow's reality.

Where you are tomorrow depends on how wisely and effectively you use the hours available today.

Start each day with a positive mental attitude.

Visualize and focus on your goals.

Carefully make your plans.

Write them down in detail.

List the things that must be done each day to accomplish your goals. Use every hour of every day to execute your plans effectively to produce desired results.

At the end of each day, ask yourself the daily question:

Did I do everything I could today to make tomorrow the way I want it to be?

When you can answer the daily question in the absolute affirmative:

Yes, I did everything I could,

with all I had to do it with!

you are well on your way to the success and achievement you seek and deserve in this lifetime.

CHAPTER ONE

HOW TO REFOCUS YOUR LIFE

The current events worldwide create a sense of uncertainty, constant change, and fear of the unknown.

How do we avoid being taken off course?

What must we do to refocus our lives in a way that will help us survive and thrive no matter what is going on in the external world?

The recent pandemic has changed how we do things in our lives, country, and world. It has changed our education, our jobs, and our social practices. Many of us are still determining how we should handle these changes.

Focus is the key to moving forward effectively.

Focus is giving or paying attention and intention to a particular desired objective or outcome.

Whatever you focus on grows.

Either you actively focus on and achieve your goals, or you fail to focus and experience whatever the world has in store for you.

There are two aspects of focus.

The first aspect of focus is time. Focus is an activity that takes place over time.

The second aspect of focus is energy. Focus is a measure of energy - a level of vibration created by desire.

Focus is the application of energy over time.

It is not an instantaneous activity that you can say, *"I did it today, and I don't have to do it again."* Focus is a continuous activity that is consistently performed over time.

There must be an objective of your focus.

You cannot be focused if you have no objective or goals.

We live in a world of vibrations and energy.

Our world exists on a spiritual energy level

that consists of vibrations. Each of us and every experience we have consists of specific vibrations. These vibrations create a force that attracts congruent things, people, experiences, and events into our lives.

These vibrations and energy are the basis of the Law of Attraction.

Whatever is presently going on in your life may be seen as a challenge, not an obstacle.

Aristotle Onassis, a shipping magnate who rose from humble beginnings to become one of the wealthiest men in the world, said,

"It is during our darkest moments that we must focus to see the light."

Focus is a powerful tool that can take you from your present condition to any desired experience or situation.

How do we lose focus?

Three ways we lose focus are:

First, we lose focus by getting into a rut.

Sometimes, we find ourselves doing the same things over and over until we don't know why we're doing them. We seem to have forgotten where we want to go – our goals and objectives.

We can get so entrenched in a rut - our comfort zone and present reality - that we no longer focus on our goals.

Second, we lose focus because of past failures and disappointments. If we go through life focusing on our failures and disappointments, it may be difficult to concentrate on finding solutions to current challenges.

Third, we lose focus when crises arise. Crises can cause distractions and make us lose focus on our goals.

In times of crisis, we must ask ourselves the refocusing questions:

"How can I use this crisis to improve my life and make it better?"

"How can I use this challenge to transform my present environment into something I desire?"

An interesting mindset in which to approach crises is to resolve that: ***"The purpose of this crisis is to allow me to show how effective I am at handling situations."***

EIGHT STEPS TO REFOCUSING YOUR LIFE

1. **Conduct a reality check.**

Your present experience with the pandemic and other external challenges is not your doing. You are alive - the same talented, intelligent person you were before these challenges occurred.

When you do a reality check and personal assessment of your thoughts, emotions, habits, and associations, remember that these challenges will not last forever. There is always a beginning and an ending to all experiences – positive or negative.

There is never a situation so dark that light does not appear.

No matter how dark the night, the sun always rises.

No matter how beautiful the sun, darkness will appear.

2. **Take responsibility for what is.**

You have the power to control your response and attitude toward the present external circumstances you are experiencing.

It is through your choices that you decide whether and to what extent you will be impacted by negativity or a crisis mentality. You have the power to see your life situation differently from the one proscribed by the crises.

The gist of the Biblical allegory of the Garden of Eden is that when humankind eats from the tree of the knowledge of good and evil, it will have the capability to make choices.

Your ability to make choices - this unique human experience - means that you must take responsibility for your choices and responses to situations that occur in your life.

Making proper choices allows you to be defined by what you desire rather than by circumstances and situations.

Take responsibility for your attitudes and your reactions. Be thoughtful and trust your ability to discern the truth.

Discerning the truth allows you to differentiate *"what is"* and act accordingly.

Identifying solutions may be challenging if you do not perfect the ability to discern and trust your common sense, instincts, and inner voice.

You must be proactive.

One aspect of confronting challenges is that there is always pushback.

You never have to plant weeds when cultivating the soil and planting flowers in a garden.

The appearance of weeds is an example of the *yin-yang* aspect of the universe. Where there is an up, there is always a down. If there is a positive, there will be a negative. Where there are flowers, weeds will appear.

You must be proactive when you are in a crisis or challenging situation. The nature of a crisis is that there is always a force that will constantly push against your efforts. You are responsible for confronting this opposing force.

A crisis makes you focus on the critical things. You push back by focusing on what is important to you.

3. **Be clear about what you do and why you do it.**

When you are in your comfort zone, you go

through the motions of doing what you usually do when you normally do it.

Sometimes, your regular actions may result from conditions that no longer exist. Examine what you are doing and why you are doing it.

Story of the ham and the pot.

An 8-year-old girl at Christmas time watched her mother cook a beautiful ham. Her mother cut off both ends of the ham before putting the ham in the pot to bake.

The little girl asked her mom, *"Why do you cut the ends of the ham before putting it in the pot to bake?"* Her mother said, *"Because my mother did it."*

Later that day, the grandmother came over for dinner, and the little girl asked her grandmother, *"Grandma, I see mom cuts the ends of the ham off before she puts it in the pot. Mom said she does it because you did it. Why do you cut the ends off the ham?"* The grandmother said, *"Because my mother did it."*

After dinner, the whole family visited the nursing home to see the great-grandmother. The little girl asked the great-grandmother the same question: " *Why did you cut the ends off the ham before you put it in the pot?* "

The great-grandmother answered, *"Because my pot was too small. "*

Although the circumstances around cutting off the ends of the ham no longer existed, the mom and grandmother kept doing it.

To refocus your life, you must examine your actions and why you do them.

You may hope for a change, but hope is not a strategy. Wishing is not a plan. You must be proactive and make things happen to facilitate change. It would help if you also learned to operate based on common sense, law, and science.

Universal, spiritual, and physical laws exist. We can often find ourselves in trouble when we violate these laws.

You must be watchful over your ego.

Be sure that your actions are not ego-centered.

Every thought creates a vibration. In times of crisis, you may assess your actions from an ego perspective. Your ego may push you to do things because you think you can or because of who you are.

When you are watchful over your ego, a vibration of truth and authenticity is created within you.

Liars may figure, but figures don't lie.

Focusing on ego-centered objectives can work against you and undermine the achievement of your goals and dreams.

In the refocusing process, you may become involved with people who are different from what you see for yourself. Associating with people who focus on the current crisis or challenge can cause you to buy into their vision.

Do not allow the wrong people into your life, especially in a crisis. Be selective about your attitude and your response to the situation.

It is not that you don't love these particular people, but you must be discerning about who you allow into your life.

Consider the story of the good Samaritan on the Golden Gate Bridge.

A good Samaritan was walking across the Golden Gate Bridge when he encountered a man in distress who was getting ready to jump off the bridge.

The good Samaritan came over and said, *"Sir, why do you want to end your life?"*

The distraught man said, "Oh, my life is terrible. It sucks." He gave a litany of horrible, negative things that were going on in his life. The good Samaritan listened intently and felt the man's pain. Then, both of them jumped off the bridge.

The moral of the story is to be cautious about letting other people's thoughts and vibrations come into your life.

Be very clear about what you do, why you do it, and with whom you do it.

4. Learn when to say yes and when to say no.

Considering the many things happening in the external world, you must be able to say no to distractions. Be deliberate in your thinking when responding to situations and challenges that confront you.

Say no to emotions of fear and to habits that

undermine your efforts to achieve your goals.

Beware of people who may not be compatible with what you are doing or where you are going.

The highest use of your power of choice is the ability to say yes or no.

5. Revisit your why.

Your why is your reason to be - your purpose. It is all you desire to be, do, and have.

Many of you start a new year with positive aspirations.

You set goals and objectives of becoming successful and experiencing the most incredible year of your life.

Then, a crisis appears, throwing you off track from pursuing your goals. This interruption and the isolation it causes provide an unexpected opportunity to revisit your why.

You can be so involved with the external world vibration that you allow the river of time to move you to where it wants you to go.

One of the benefits of social isolation is that you have an opportunity to meet and spend time with yourself.

Your deeper, personal awareness cannot be experienced, heard, or felt when noise – external activities surround you.

The essence of life is energy and vibration. When you can be still and know, you have a better environment to revisit your why.

One of the reasons that virtually every religion or spiritual discipline uses meditation is that outside vibrations and interference must be silenced to hear the inner voice of wisdom, truth, and clarity.

This inner voice of wisdom, truth, and clarity gives you the insight to recognize the power you possess to handle external situations and crises.

When you listen to your inner voice, you can reflect on the greatness of who you are and the gift you can give to the world.

The Biblical allegory of Paul and Silas.

Paul and Silas were two followers of Jesus. They were placed deep in prison for preaching the gospel. After prayer and singing while bound in their cell, an earthquake flung open the jail doors. Paul and Silas were freed to continue preaching the gospel and pursuing their purpose.

A crisis can be like an earthquake - a wake-up call to focus on the essence of being you and the purpose for which you were created.

Ask yourself two questions:

1. ***What good lessons must I learn from this crisis?***
2. ***What important activities should I undertake based on these lessons?***

In revisiting your why, consider how you can use your current situation to reintroduce yourself and listen to your inner voice.

Acknowledge that a crisis can make you better. In fact, a crisis can reveal or magnify who you already are. Sometimes, a challenge is necessary to show you the tremendous power you possess.

When you operate in your comfort zone, you are not really challenged. However, when you experience a great crisis, the energy and vibrations you create push against that situation, magnifying who you are and helping you refocus on your goals, vision, and purpose.

You can now redefine your why as you listen to your inner self and allow your essence to emerge. This process reveals that you were created for a purpose that resonates with you and attracts what you desire.

6. **Establish priorities based on your new why.**

Priority is the foundation of choice. Establishing new priorities requires choosing how to allocate your time, energy, and resources.

Priority is the guiding mechanism for focus. Focusing on what's important allows you to determine the best use of your time and create the new *'why'* you have defined for yourself.

7. **Take action.**

Action is the execution of focus. Focus is the application of energy over time.

Without action, nothing happens. People may have time and be excited and enthusiastic, but nothing happens if they do not take action.

Action is where the rubber hits the road - where focus and energy are applied.

8. **Keep going and growing.**

The process of going and growing expands the vibrations that you send out to the universe.

When you keep going and growing, you build confidence by focusing over time.

Faith guides the vibration of focused energy over time.

Faith – the substance of things hoped for and the evidence of things not seen - gives direction to the energy of focus.

When you increase your vibration level through focused desire, the things you seek manifest in your life.

Don't worry about how things manifest in your life. Do the work, and the results will appear.

It is a lot like having a baby. A man and a woman can physically come together to create a life, but the creator – the God mind - is the *'how'* that makes it happen.

We don't understand how to make a heartbeat or a blood vessel. The man and the woman do their part – put in the time and energy. The creator takes care of the how.

The nature of the creative spirit is that if you put in the time, work, and energy, the how will take care of itself.

CHAPTER SUMMARY

You can handle obstacles and crises by refocusing your life on your desires and dreams.

The eight steps to refocusing your life can take you from where you are to wherever you desire to be.

Do not allow external circumstances to impact the choices you make. You have the ability to do what must be done to create the life of your dreams.

Conduct a personal reality check. Understand what is happening and who you are.

Take responsibility for what is. Create the thoughts, emotions, habits, and relationships that will take you from where you are to wherever you want to go, no matter what.

You have the capacity to understand the actions that must be taken, why they must be taken, and what you must focus on.

Avoid things that are not necessary and focus

on the important things.

Say yes or no to make proper choices in response to the situations or crises that confront you.

Revisit your why. Take time to be still and know - based on your reality check - what is truly important to you and your vision.

Establish new priorities that create new vibrations to attract whatever you seek into your life.

Take action. Action is positive proof of your desire. The focus of your energy over time will produce the desired results.

Keep going and growing, knowing that you can create a world exactly how you want it to be.

When you choose the right thoughts, feelings, actions, and associations, you can be what you want to be, do what you want to do, and have whatever you desire, regardless of what's happening around you.

Using these steps to refocus your life will create the life experience of your dreams.

GREATEST VICTORY CONTRIBUTOR JAY CLARK

Background:

I was raised in New York City.

After High School, I realized I needed to get into a trade.

I decided to pursue a five-year electrical apprenticeship program.

Getting into the union:

When I started pursuing a career as an electrician, I realized that very few people – especially black people – successfully completed the apprenticeship programs. Many people of color felt that they were not wanted in the union.

I took the electrician's test and passed it.

After passing the test, I went through an interview process.

There was a five-person interview panel, and

they had one question for us.

"Why do you want to become an electrician?

If your primary objective was the money you could make, that could be a no-no.

Fortunately, I was tutored on how to handle the interview. I spoke about liking to work with electricity and always doing a good job.

I also had to write a 100-word essay on why I wanted to become an electrician.

One of the interviewers looked at my essay and then asked the same question.

They wanted to know if I had written it or whether someone else had written it for me.

Another interviewer asked me: *"If your mechanic told you to dig a ditch to lay down some pipes for insulation, would you do it?"*

I answered yes. He continued, *"Why would you do it?"*

Thanks to my coaching at ***Fight Back***, I knew how to handle it. ***Fight Back*** was an organization that helped young people through the apprenticeship process.

I answered, *"First, he's my instructor - my coach. I am here to learn. I would do what he told me to do."*

If I had answered, *"That's not my job,"* I would probably have failed the interview.

During my first year in the union, I didn't get much work in the shops. They didn't want me there. The shops would cater to other folks that looked like them. When I would come in wanting to learn, they would turn their backs on me. Sometimes, I felt hostility.

Life Lesson:

One of the things that I learned was that when you have challenges, it can make you grow.

One of the critical aspects of getting into the union and completing my apprenticeship was the importance of having help – a mentor who could show the way. ***Fight Back*** was my mentor.

Fight Back was an organization that helped minorities get the correct type of information and coaching to get into the electrician's or plumbers' unions. The counselors there told me to stay focused and avoid getting into any conflict or controversy.

That's what I did. Some young people would like to get into the trade unions. If nobody guides them, it could be challenging. In the end, it was all worth it. I had a great career and was awarded a pension based on 50 years of service and a gold watch.

God was the light that guided me through these challenges to focus on the future.

I may have to eat some crud for a while. But keep a good temperament. In the end, it was worth it.

A time I wanted to quit:

There was a time when I wanted to quit. I was on a job as an apprentice working in New York City at the post office on 30th Street. I was told to clean up the bathrooms.

One of the bosses said, *"You work for me. Do what I tell you."*

He harassed me. That's when I said to myself, "This is crazy."

"This ain't worth it. These folks don't want me to succeed," I said to myself.

But I had a friend - a woman whose brother

was in the union. She said,

"You did not come into this trade for a haircut. You came here for a purpose.

Right now, they are carrying a big stick. You may have to eat a little crud.

But your job is to do whatever it takes to be successful."

My ego had to subside. I had to change my attitude.

One of the mechanics on the job told me that "even when he's wrong, he was right."

That's when I decided to learn and apply myself.

My Goals:

My goal was to take care of my family. I was a young father at that time.

I wanted to learn as much as I could and share it with others.

You must be able to dream - to go into the theatre of your mind.

I knew that there was something bigger and

better out there.

I never forgot that my mother always told me that you can make it as long as you have your health, strength, and mind.

Whenever I got to the point where I felt like throwing up my hands and quitting, I remembered what my mother said. Winners never quit, and quitters never win.

During that time, I met Dr. Herbert Harris and his associate Tiamo Rauf and their ***"Will Power, Build Power"*** personal development program. They were teaching success and how to achieve it. I completed the class, and it was life changing.

One of the things that I learned from reading ***The Twelve Universal Laws of Success*** was that you will have challenges and be tested.

I realized that to win in life, I must learn to overcome challenges.

My main takeaway was don't ever quit, no matter what,

Goliath Moment:

My Goliath moment came when I realized

that I never really looked at Jay Clark and what I was truly about. It was when I realized that what I was doing was not the best for my life.

As a matter of fact, it was detrimental. I needed to change.

I realized that God had brought me that far, but to go to the next level, I have to change.

I had a few death and life situations. I was being tested. God was knocking on my door, giving me opportunities to change.

But I was very stubborn - procrastinating about changing.

I finally realized that I had to die for that old self.

God was telling me to take time to reflect on my life and ask for guidance.

I told my wife at that time that what I was doing was not in alignment with my best self.

A voice inside told me I was no good - why don't you end it all?

I was in a dark place. I said to myself, this is not the truth of me.

But I had to be still to hear what God was saying and then make adjustments. Each of us comes to a realization when we assess our situation and be honest with ourselves.

Be true to yourself.

When you look into your mirror, you have to be true to yourself. You can hide from others, but you cannot hide from yourself. When you look in the mirror, sometimes you don't like what you see.

I looked at myself in the mirror and did not like what I saw.

That's when I knew I had to change.

Handling Distractions:

One of my distractions was chasing skirts. In the disco era, when everything was moving fast, I had a lot of friends who were single and partying.

My friends would say let's go party. I got distracted from my home life by just wanting to be out at the party in the disco. I got away from having a teacher, a mentor, someone who could show me there's a better way.

What got me through:

Understanding my spirituality helped me come to grips with being a Christian.

I remembered the principles that my mother and father taught me. I had to go back to my roots, be still, and ask God to guide me.

Greatest Victory:

My greatest victory was coming to the understanding of who I am in God in Christ.

I needed a solid foundation. In my construction days as an electrician, we knew that if we were working on a building, it had to have the proper footings that go deep into the earth's foundation to hit bedrock.

Depending on how high that building was, the foundation beams had to be dug deep down to the bedrock. We are here for a purpose. – like a seed planted to grow.

In order to grow into your greatest potential, you have to die to your old self.

My greatest victory is realizing that I am still growing and pursuing my purpose.

Every day, I am going and growing - learning

more and more about who Jay is.

Final thoughts:

I needed to look at myself in the mirror and say, *"Who am I?"*

Stay plugged into someone who can lift you up.

Someone you can talk to and be able to hear a good word.

Dr. Herbert Harris has been a good friend for over 35 years.

He shared insights with me when I felt down or discouraged, which lifted me up to keep going and growing.

Biography and Contact Information of Jay Clark:

"Your health is your wealth."

Jay Clark has been happily involved in the health and wellness Industry for over 40 years. He is a certified seed-based nutritional advisor, success educator, home-based business owner, and certified reboundologist.

Jay's main objective Is to help people change their lives physically & financially. He shows people how to cleanse and detoxify the trillions of cells in their bodies. The Mini-Rebounder is his tool to re-energize the cellular cleansing process.

The "Health Is Wealth System" is based on the seven steps to a high-level wellness model. Learning about and strengthening your Immune system and oxygenating the body is essential.

Don't hesitate to contact me if you want to change your life by strengthening your Immune system and shedding pounds from your belly, thighs, and hips.

Call 917-721-7832 for free consultation. More information is available on my website: www.Healthalljay.com

GREATEST VICTORY CONTRIBUTOR CASSANDRA HENDERSON

Background:

As a young girl, I always sensed that there was much more to life, and I had a deep curiosity for something beyond what I knew.

After getting married and having my children, I felt a new sense of urgency to discover my purpose, so I immersed myself in personal development activities. My curiosity led me to read books like *The Twelve Universal Laws of Success.* Hearing the stories of other entrepreneurs convinced me that I could also be successful.

After spending fifteen years in the corporate world, I realized I needed to follow my entrepreneurial calling. I established a digital solutions company specializing in building lead generation systems for small businesses. I just needed to start. Today, I am on my way to becoming a full-time entrepreneur.

Ten years after I had the idea, I launched my personal development and leadership platform for women called *Growth Focused Nation.* This program helps women stand in their leadership, take charge of their lives, and achieve success.

Life Lessons and Overcoming Obstacles:

One of my biggest challenges has been navigating the part-time entrepreneurship journey. I embarked on this path when my second daughter was born. While I was excited about starting a business, not having a plan or structure made life especially challenging.

I experienced many feelings of guilt and the weight of not being present as a mother. My focus was on providing for the family's needs, so it became a struggle to find balance. In contrast, I still needed a clear direction.

During tough times when I feel like giving up, my husband's belief in me and my faith in God helps me to maintain the relentless pursuit of greatness. I am constantly reminded that abundance is my birthright. If I'm not experiencing it, I still need to do work to be aligned.

What is Your Greatest Passion and Victory?

I have a sweet spot for helping women realize their full potential and life purpose. I've dedicated myself to building the *Growth Focused Nation* community and advancing my digital solutions company.

Many people's frustrations in achieving their dreams stem from not making the decision to step into their personal leadership. Our community focuses on bridging the gap between aspiring entrepreneurs and those who are already successful.

We aim to offer strategic, intensive workshops focused on shaping the mindset and providing the necessary business and personal development tools for individuals to become leaders in their own lives.

The Twelve Universal Laws of Success has played a significant role in shaping my mindset. It was the mental conditioning my mind, spirit, and body needed to prepare me for action.

This book gave me the structure I needed to create a solid plan to realize my dreams.

What message would you give to people seeking success in their lives?

My word to people seeking success would be to do their inner work. Everything starts with inner clarity and a decision. Take the time you need to decide, especially if you're uncertain about which path to choose. You may find that the dream or vision you're considering is not as enticing or stimulating as you thought. In such cases, pause and reflect until your path becomes clear.

Invest time in personal development and do whatever it takes to condition and prepare your mind to make a decision. The growth that occurs in the pursuit of a goal is transformative, regardless of whether you reach that specific goal. It shapes your mindset, teaches you to shed baggage, reveals opportunities, builds relationships, and empowers you on your journey. Once you have made your decision, let nothing and no one deter you.

Biography and Contact Information:

Cassandra Henderson is an IT consultant in Software Engineering, Business Intelligence, Data Management, and Marketing.

Her core philosophy is that unlocking innate

leadership qualities through self-awareness and authenticity is the key to creating a life and business aligned with your purpose.

Cassandra is a highly sought-after leadership coach and transformational communicator. She is the founder of *Growth Focus® Academy*. This online learning community empowers women to stand in their authentic leadership and create their own opportunities for life fulfillment.

Because of her life challenges, she is on a mission to help women stand in their truth and be more, do more, and experience more in every area of their lives.

Cassandra is the producer and host of THE SAN SCRIPTS® Podcast, where she shares valuable insights on practical approaches to growth and cultivating the TRUE self.

She resides in South Georgia as a wife, author, and mother of two wonderful children.

To learn more or to work with Cassandra, visit: www.thecassandrahenderson.com

Email: info@thecassandrahenderson.com

Mailing address: Cassandra Henderson, 3379 Peachtree Road NE, Suite 655-C10, Atlanta, GA 30326

SUCCESS HONOR ROLL

Derek Phillips is the founder and CEO of the **Real Dads Network**, a non-profit organization dedicated to fortifying the family by showcasing the positive facets of fathers through all forms of media.

Derek and his wife Maria have been married for over 27 years and have two daughters, Jordyn and Maya. They inspire him to push the boundaries of positive fatherhood.

As a retired Assistant Principal with over 27 years in the New York City Department of Education, Derek has interacted with fathers and parents on many levels.

The Real Dads Network grew out of Derek Phillips' award-winning documentary, **"Real Dads – Black Men on Fatherhood,"** which he produced and co-directed. This documentary, featuring the legendary actor Ossie Davis, focused on positive black fathers, shattering stereotypes, and breaking barriers.

Real Dads Network: Empowering Fatherhood Through Community and Advocacy

Real Dads Network's vision is to strengthen the family by offering fathers support, valuable information, essential resources, and transformative opportunities. The empowerment of fathers is pivotal for the well-being of families and communities.

Walking the Journey Together

Real Dads Network invites fathers and families to join this transformative journey. With a wealth of resources, engaging events, and camaraderie, the network is a compass for fathers navigating the uncharted waters of fatherhood.

Contact Information:

Real Dads Network

P.O. Box 125

Peekskill, NY 10566

Phone: 212-875-7725

Email: admin@realdadsnetwork.org

Website: www.realdadsnetwork.org

CHAPTER TWO

HOW TO OVERCOME SELF-DOUBT

Self-doubt is an experience that happens to most of us at some point in our lives. It is a feeling of insecurity that we are not good enough or don't have what it takes to accomplish a particular outcome.

When making decisions, self-doubt can creep in, making us unsure of ourselves or questioning whether what we are doing is what we should be doing.

Self-doubt is worse than procrastination. With procrastination, you may put off until tomorrow what should have been done yesterday. Self-doubt can stop you in your tracks and undermine everything you are attempting to do so that you don't get anything accomplished.

William Shakespeare said,

"Our doubts are traitors, and make us lose

the good we oft might win by fearing to attempt."

Self-doubt can paralyze you and stop you from accomplishing the things you desire – something that you are otherwise capable of achieving.

Life is like a river.

We live in a world that is constantly changing and transforming. Life can be seen as a great river continuously flowing into the sea of eternity.

We are like ships navigating the river of time by our choices and actions.

When we allow self-doubt to paralyze us into inaction, we are swept along the river of time by the prevailing currents rather than by our own choices. These currents active on the river of time may be positive or negative. By not taking action because of self-doubt, the ship that is our lives goes wherever the river takes it.

Self-doubt causes hesitation.

I love watching basketball games with a few seconds left, and someone needs to take that last shot to win or lose the game.

Certain players, experiencing self-doubt, pass the ball rather than take the game-winning shot. Other players permit self-doubt to enter their minds, causing hesitation - just a fraction of a second – that makes them lose their rhythm and miss the shot.

Michael Jordan, one of the greatest basketball players of all time, said,

"I have missed more than 9,000 shots in my career. I've lost almost 300 games, 26 times, I've been trusted to take the game-winning shot and missed. I've failed over and over and over again in my life. And that is why I succeed."

Self-doubt can undermine everything you are attempting to do. Allowing a moment of doubt to creep in can throw off your rhythm for success. If self-doubt is so devastating – and it is – how do you overcome it?

TEN KEYS TO OVERCOME SELF-DOUBT

1. Recognizing Doubt is a Negative Emotion.

The first key to overcoming self-doubt is to realize that doubt is a negative emotion.

Doubt is a weed. If you permit it to grow, it will consume your garden.

An experienced gardener is always looking for and pulling up weeds. If you do not pull up the weeds, they will consume your garden.

Self-doubt is a negative emotion, a weed you must constantly pull up. Every thought has an emotional aspect associated with it. The emotional part of a thought is a seed from which the thought grows and becomes real.

When the seed is planted in the garden of your consciousness, it will always manifest. When you plant positive seeds - good ideas, emotions, habits, and relationships, you create flowers – positive manifestations.

On the other hand, if you plant negative seeds like self-doubt in your consciousness, they will also manifest in accord with their nature – negative manifestations.

It is interesting to note that when you plant seeds – positive or negative - weeds will appear. You don't have to plant weeds. Self-doubt undermines your efforts because you are, in effect, growing weeds.

How do we pull up or stop planting weeds – negative emotions?

We must reprogram our minds. Negative self-talk is a major cause of self-doubt. We plant seeds of self-doubt when we say things to ourselves like *"I don't have what it takes"* or *"I can't do this."*

Anytime you are confronted with the weed of self-doubt, pull it up and neutralize it by saying, *"That's not for me."*

Self-talk is a powerful tool to neutralize self-doubt. Athletes do it to pump themselves up and create a victory.

When sports teams face a challenge, they huddle together, repeating, *"We can do it! We can do it! We can fight the fight!"*

We remember the **"Little Engine That Could"** saying, *"I think I can! I think I can! I think I can!"*

We can program our minds and life experiences by telling our minds what to think. When weeds enter your mind, and self-doubt tries to manifest, say and feel, *"That's not for me!"*

2. Review the Past

The second key to overcoming self-doubt is to review your past.

Be aware that whatever you seek, you will find. Very often, self-doubt is based on past failures or disappointments. If you review your past and focus on the negative things that occurred, you can confirm or validate the self-doubt. This negative approach creates a failure consciousness that affirms, *"I can't do it,"* or *"Maybe this is not for me."*

Can you imagine Thomas Edison after he had failed over 3000 times to find a filament for the light bulb? If he had permitted self-doubt to dwell in his consciousness, Edison would have probably quit and stopped looking for the filament.

Then, someone else would have discovered the light bulb. Once an idea's time has come, if one person doesn't act on it, that idea passes on to someone else.

Thomas Edison reprogrammed his mind by saying, *"I have never failed at anything, but I have successfully identified 3000 ways it will not work."*

Winston Churchill, Prime Minister of

England during World War II, said, *"Success is going from failure to failure without loss of enthusiasm."*

You must be able to fail and yet keep your enthusiasm for success. Be mindful whenever self-doubt tries to enter your mind. Always look for past positive outcomes where you were victorious and find strength there. Once you've done that, write, *"I have been victorious in the past!"*

This reprogramming of the mind helps to neutralize the emotion of doubt.

3. Talk to Someone.

The third key is to talk to someone else about your challenge.

Michael Jordan grew up and attended school in Wilmington, North Carolina. He was not that tall - he's only 6' 6" - and not particularly great at basketball. But he had something special inside that radiated, *"I am the greatest; I can do it!"*

I'm sure there were times when he couldn't hit the side of a barn with the ball, but he had a coach who worked with him.

When seeking help, look for somebody who's

been where you are and faced the same or similar challenges you're now facing. Ask them, *"How did you overcome that situation when all seemed lost? What made you get up and fight another round?"*

Consider Muhammad Ali and his *"Rumble in the Jungle"* fight against George Foreman. Ali understood he was not in top shape, but knew he was fighting for the championship.

So, what did Ali do? He probably said to himself, *"I'll outlast him. I'll let George Foreman punch himself out until he has nothing left, and then I'll dispense with him."*

If you want to win, don't lose, no matter what. All you have to do is not go down because, sooner or later, your opponent will wear themselves out. And then you win.

When you get help, be careful not to seek someone who has never played the game. Speak to someone who has been where you want to go and can show you the way. Talking to the wrong people can confirm your self-doubt.

Avoid people who confirm your past failures or commiserate by sharing their own shortcomings.

Be selective with whom you share your doubts and who can help.

Surround yourself with positive people who have accomplished or been through more situations than you have. Seek out people who know more than you and have been to places you want to go.

Surround yourself with people who can guide you when you need counsel or someone to talk to.

If you are the smartest person in a group, you are in the wrong group.

4. Write it Down.

The fourth key to overcoming self-doubt is to write it down.

Writing is a powerful tool to improve clarity. Whatever your situation may be, write it down and describe it in detail.

For example, suppose you want to be a motivational speaker, but you are scared and get butterflies in your stomach when it's time to walk out onto the stage. Write every aspect of your thoughts and feelings immediately before it's time to speak.

If you become paralyzed when confronted with a challenge and there's a tendency to doubt, ask yourself, *"Why am I afraid to go out on the stage?"*

Are you afraid you will lose your place, or will you forget what you have to say? Maybe you believe you will not connect with the audience or that you won't inspire them. Once you write your thoughts and feelings about public speaking, you will begin to see that it isn't that bad.

I remember watching a speaker at a conference with over 5,000 people in the audience. When the speaker came onto the stage, he became so paralyzed with fear that he could not speak. Finally, his friend walked onto the stage and put their arm around him. With the encouragement of his friend, the speaker was able to talk, and the audience responded with enthusiastic applause.

French philosopher Michel de Montaigne once said,

"My life has been filled with terrible misfortunes, most of which never happened."

Once you write the thoughts and feelings causing your doubt, you convert a vague feeling of doubt into specific thoughts and feelings that can be addressed.

For example, if you are fearful that the audience won't like you, remind yourself that you have already been paid.

If you are concerned about losing your place, remember you can wing it. No one knows what you're going to say anyway. The audience won't know if you leave out some key points.

Writing these concerns down helps remove the fear or trepidation you may experience.

Power Technique

Keep a record in a notebook or planner of the good things you accomplish at the end of every day. Write down the tasks that were completed, the good people you met, and the good experiences you had or performed that day.

When you have a moment of self-doubt, review your notes and remember that you had challenges before and overcame them.

You've been there, done that, and have a T-shirt to prove it.

Now you can move on. Your list of past

accomplishments will form a powerful reminder of your strength and inspire you to future achievements.

5. Overcome Other People's Expectations.

The fifth key to overcoming self-doubt is to ignore or overcome other people's expectations.

My dad was a great philosopher of life. He had no degrees, and he didn't read very well. But he had common sense and did his best to teach me.

He said, ***"People don't care about your situation. Don't share your problems with people. Half of them don't care, and the other half are glad you have the problem."***

Overcoming self-doubt is recognizing that most people don't care about your situation. Accepting this mindset will free you from being chained by other people's expectations.

If you're a speaker, when you walk out on the stage, say to yourself,

"Let her rip! I'm going for it!"

There is great power in choosing freedom and not letting other people's expectations become the chain that holds you down. Once you realize that, what other people say, think, or do does not affect you. You are free.

"People who can't fly criticize those who can."

"People who cannot dance don't understand those who can hear the music."

6. Appeal to a Higher Power.

The sixth key to overcoming self-doubt is to appeal to a higher power or authority.

Go to a higher authority when challenged with critical decisions and wonder whether you are doing it right or have what it takes.

Renowned physicist Albert Einstein said,

"We cannot solve our problems with the same thinking we used when we created them."

Going to a higher authority can mean coming together with people who have been where you are trying to go. Form a friendly alliance with intelligent, experienced people who care about you and wish to help you succeed.

The mastermind principle provides that when two or more are gathered on one accord, I AM among them. I AM is the making power – the alignment of your conscious, subconscious, and superconscious minds that facilitates access to the source or the God mind. Accessing the power of the mastermind, all things are possible.

If you are feeling down, defeated, and unsure of yourself, surround yourself with people who inspire you and bring you clarity.

When people face challenges, they often read a particular Bible passage, such as the 23rd Psalm, to find encouragement and comfort.

Listening to motivational messages or reading success books helps you overcome the challenge.

Art Williams, founder of AL Williams Insurance Company, created a powerful speech entitled *"Just do it."*

Art's message was, no matter what the challenge, "Just do it."

Even if it's a rainy day and no one shows up for a meeting, *"Just do it."*

If the crowd around you tells you it's impossible, don't worry about it. *"Just do it!"*

The appeal to a higher authority can inspire you or change your state of mind and uplift you when you doubt yourself.

7. **All Setbacks are Temporary.**

The seventh key to overcoming self-doubt is to realize that all setbacks are temporary, regardless of how bad they seem.

No matter how dark the night, the day always comes.

Weeds may grow unchecked in your garden. But when you take a rake and hoe and pull up those weeds, you can rectify the situation and restore your beautiful garden.

Sometimes, when we experience a setback, its purpose is to stimulate our growth and prepare us for the next level.

We are like diamonds that must be tested and put under pressure to bring out our brilliant shine – our possibilities for success.

The difference between a diamond and a piece of coal is pressure. The chemical composition of a piece of coal and a diamond is basically the same. But a diamond is a piece of coal that has been put under extreme pressure.

When you experience setbacks, it may be the pressure you need to force your growth to become the winner that you are.

Motivational speaker Willie Jolly says, ***"Every setback is just a setup for a comeback."***

8. Sharpen Your Skills.

The eighth key to overcoming self-doubt is to sharpen your skills.

As we go through life, we learn what we are good at and not so good at. Sometimes, the moment of self-doubt is based on your lack of skill. Whenever you believe there is something you're not good at, work on improving your skill level in that particular area.

A friend, one of the top network marketing speakers in the industry, told me that she was a little nervous and had to practice before an upcoming engagement.

I asked her, *"You are one of the top speakers. Why would you practice?"*

She said, *"Because I always want to grow my skill level."*

When you constantly sharpen your skills, you are committed to being and doing better. This pursuit of excellence creates a vibration within that makes you open and receptive to learning new things and growing your skill level.

Your confidence grows as your skill level expands and your self-doubt is neutralized.

9. Don't Beat Yourself Up.

The ninth key to overcoming self-doubt is to never beat yourself up.

You may be confronted with decisions or situations where you doubt yourself, especially If you have made wrong decisions in the past and things did not work out the way you thought they would.

Don't stress or beat yourself up. Consider every experience – good or bad – as a learning experience.

Beating yourself up destroys your initiative and compounds the negativity of failure. It is like a farmer who plants weeds in his garden that will eventually consume it.

Recognize that everything happens for a purpose. You either succeed or learn. Either way, you're better off.

10. You Can Course Correct.

The tenth key is that you can always course correct.

Success isn't permanent, and failure isn't final. Success is the continuous realization of a worthwhile purpose. Failure is a constant learning process to help you get better.

We are where we are in our lives as a result of our thoughts, emotions, actions, and relationships.

The fact that you can always course-correct allows for creating new outcomes.

The second law of success states, *"Be not conformed to this world."*.

Whatever situation or challenge you're confronted with right now, you don't have to stay there. You can be *"transformed by the renewing of your mind."*

Reprogram your consciousness and change the outcomes you experience in life by taking control of your thoughts, emotions, actions, and relationships.

Couple this reprogramming with self-discipline and persistence, and nothing is impossible.

Vincent Van Gogh had great insight into self-doubt. He said,

"If you hear a voice within, say you cannot paint, then paint by all means, and that voice will be silenced."

CHAPTER SUMMARY

Most people are confronted with self-doubt at some point in their lives.

Faith is the substance of things hoped for and the evidence of things not seen. Doubt can undermine faith. Faith can neutralize doubt.

Using the **Ten Keys to Overcome Self-Doubt** will provide a foundation for better decision-making, neutralizing doubt and replacing it with faith.

1. Recognize doubt for what it is, a negative emotion - a weed in the garden of life.

2. Look into your past for the positive actions you have taken and the positive outcomes you created. This introspection can change your frame of reference from failure to success.

3. Talk with someone who has been there: faced the challenges you are experiencing and overcame them.

4. Write down clearly and concisely the details of whatever situation is causing you to doubt

yourself. Describe how it makes you feel - doubt, fear, or uneasiness.

5. Overcome other people's expectations. Realize that most people don't care about what happens to you. Free yourself from other people's opinions, expectations, or criticism.

6. Appeal to a higher authority. Always have someone or something you can go to for encouragement or inspiration to take you to the next level.

7. Recognize that all setbacks are temporary. No matter how dark the night, the light will come.

8. Sharpen your skills so that you can get better every day, in every way.

9. Don't beat yourself up no matter what. Realize that every experience is for a purpose.

10. Remember that you can always course correct.

If you hear a voice within that makes you doubt yourself and your ability to do something, take action and do it anyway. That voice of self-doubt will be silenced. Action neutralizes doubt.

These ten keys can help you overcome self-doubt and put you in a position to write your goals, make plans, and take action.

Every time you hear a negative comment or self-doubt tries to creep into your life, say and feel, "***That's not for me.***"

Spread your wings and fly to your dreams. You can be, do, or have anything you desire by taking action with confidence and faith. Stick to the task until it is done - always knowing that the best is yet to come.

GREATEST VICTORY CONTRIBUTOR TONYA DEBNAM

Background:

My name is Tonya Debnam, and I am a native of Raleigh, North Carolina. I was raised in a large family with eight siblings, the seventh of nine children. I graduated from the University of North Carolina at Greensboro, then moved to Atlanta to live and work for about seven years.

I realized my family dynamics were unique. Growing up, I never lived with neighbors that were not family. My neighbors were my aunts, uncles, cousins, and grandparents. My grandfather owned land and gave all eleven of his children land to build their homes.

Getting into Banking:

My introduction to a career in banking started after I graduated college. I wasn't happy with my job in Atlanta, and I asked myself,

*"What do you want to do? What do you feel passionate about?" B*anking kept showing up, so I decided to interview for a job in banking, and they hired me. I started my banking career in Georgia and finished it in Raleigh.

When I started my career in banking, there were very few minorities employed. I joined a banking minority organization called NAUB, the National Association of Urban Bankers. We supported each other and would host national and local chapter conferences. This organization gave us opportunities to network.

Networking makes a big difference because you connect with people outside your regular group. It also allows you to create relationships and mentorships. Those relationships gave me people and resources to support me through challenging situations. They made my career better and more enjoyable.

Many people don't go into the banking industry because they don't necessarily see the opportunities. Opportunities definitely exist, but how many people encourage their children to enter banking? I have encouraged and helped people get into banking, using the connections I've made over almost 20 years in the industry -

and they've enjoyed the journey.

My Shift to Real Estate:

I worked in the banking industry for a long time before deciding to try something different. That's when I got into real estate. I started in real estate nearly fifteen years ago.

A National Association of Realtors report on home ownership in America was released in 2023. It states that the racial group with the highest homeownership rate is white Americans. Their rate of homeownership is 73%. The next race is Asian Americans, with a homeownership rate of 63%. The next group is Hispanic Americans, with a rate of about 53%. The African American rate of home ownership is at 42%.

These statistics are very frustrating and emotionally taxing for me because African Americans are the only race where homeownership rates decreased from 2010 to 2020. We must do a lot of education to change our numbers.

I can relate to a quote for the low homeownership rate: *"Your ignorance is their power."*

We learn so many things in school: algebra, trigonometry, history - which is important. But we need to be taught about homeownership. That is very important to our lives. Homeownership brings more wealth to your net worth than anything else.

Gentrification is occurring throughout African American communities. You do not hear of this happening in other communities - like areas known as *Chinatown.* I believe this gentrification is happening because many African Americans don't take complete ownership of everything in our communities.

When you go to Chinatown, they own everything. They own the businesses, the real estate, and pretty much everything. Thus, it is not easy to come in and take over.

Life Lessons & Overcoming Obstacles:

I am a single mom with one child. That was probably one of my biggest challenges in life. Being a single mother and a business owner is hard. Sometimes, I thought I had chosen the most challenging route on the planet by doing both simultaneously.

Tonya was another obstacle I had to

overcome. I had to get out of my own way and believe in myself. When I reflected on my life and did self-love, I realized Tonya is a beautiful person, and she has done great things.

I've been a cheerleader all my life, throughout middle and high school. I cheered in college, and now I am a cheerleader for life. I became a cheerleader for everybody except Tonya.

Using Dr. Harris' book, *The Twelve Universal Laws of Success*, taught me about self-love and self-reflection.

The Covid pandemic period gave me the time I needed to slow down and reassess what I was doing with my life. I had been busy doing things but not reflecting on what I was doing or why I was doing it. These experiences helped me overcome the other great obstacles in my life.

My Passion and Greatest Victory:

My friends tease me because they know I'm passionate about many things. I'm passionate about our people learning the value of real estate: how to get property, maintain it, and keep it.

I have always wanted to write a book called *"The M.O. Never Changes."* We need to understand the M.O. – Method of Operation - and how it affects us.

We created Black Wall Streets and other wealth-building opportunities, and then the power structure came in and tore them down.

The mastermind concept must exist to avoid another Black Wall Street, where you know they will come after you. This arrangement is where the next generation develops those mastermind groups, so we are prepared to protect ourselves when the power structure comes after us.

We know that energy cannot be created or destroyed. It can only be transferred or transformed. Until the consciousness that created America has been transformed, it will always be here. Part of the Mastermind focus is how to become a transformer, change negative energy into positive energy, and create something better for the world.

I love people, and I enjoy helping people achieve their goals. Learning to love Tonya and having my daughter are two of my greatest victories. I would love this young woman whether she was my daughter or not.

I have made many sacrifices so that my

daughter can be the great contributor to the world that she is and will be. She's a beautiful spirit, and I hope I had much to do with that.

My mom believed that children should be seen and not heard. When you go to church, they can see you, but they should never hear you, which stuck with me. Now that I am a mature woman, I refuse to remain silent.

Is There Any Particular Chapter In The Twelve Universal Laws Of Success You Prefer?

Chapter One, the Law of Thought. As a woman of color growing up in America, I did not see examples of persons who looked like me in leadership positions. I knew I could not be the only one to experience low self-esteem. I had to deal with feelings of being unworthy. In my opinion, the black woman is still at the bottom. The Law of Thought is the chapter that touches my soul and the one that resonates most with me.

What message would you give to people seeking success in their lives?

Have a vision and build a team. In my first business, I didn't have a business plan. The third law of success in the book is the Law of Vision. I would never do business again without a business plan.

Vision requires that you have a team. That team should comprise people with strengths in areas that are not your expertise. People usually get into business in their area of strength, but you should hire or build relationships with people with strengths in your weak areas.

Spend time with and listen to your children. Have a spiritual background that they can connect to. When I decided what to teach my child, I wanted an integrated church where everyone was welcome and not segregated. I found churches with that foundation, background, and connection that worked well for us.

One of the things I call myself is a transformer. Energy cannot be created or destroyed. It can only be transformed or transferred. I consider myself a transformer because my job is to transform others into something more significant and show them that negative thoughts could be a lie.

My philosophy:

If you've heard something from multiple people about yourself, it's time to do some self-reflection.

Before you can solve a problem, you must admit you have a problem.

Don't present a problem unless you've thought about a solution.

I learned that lesson when I first started my career in banking. I had a mentor, and she said, *"Before you come to complain about something, think about the problem, and don't bring a complaint without bringing some kind of solution for it as well."*

That worked my whole life, and I told my daughter the same thing. Don't come to me with a complaint without thinking about a solution we can work through together.

I love people. And I am willing to share my wisdom with those who want help and guidance. Les Brown said, *"...in the graveyard is where you will find all the events that never happened and information or wisdom that was never shared."*

I refuse to go to the graveyard without sharing the knowledge I've gained from my banking and real estate careers and my life experiences.

Biography and Contact Information for Tony Debnam

AuntT also known as Tonya Debnam is a consummate professional. She has over 30 years of experience in the financial industry and specialized real estate knowledge. She is a native of Raleigh, North Carolina, and a graduate of the University of North Carolina at Greensboro.

Currently, Tonya is the author of a book titled *"Mama Said"* and Principal of *Golden Sun Enterprises (GSE),* a full-service Real Estate business. She also founded a non-profit organization, *Self-Educated Revolution (SER).*

During *AuntT's* 20-year corporate call, she acquired vast business knowledge. Her professional drive and personal initiative led her to acquire her Series 6 and 63 investment licenses. During her corporate calling, Tonya has a Real Estate Agent, Real Estate Broker, and Mortgage Loan Officer License.

Email: tonyadebnam@gmail.com

Website: www.mamasaid.live

GREATEST VICTORY CONTRIBUTOR PRINCESS CASTLEBERRY

I was born and raised by the hardest working teen mother on Detroit's West Side. My father was a budding - and now famed - bass player and music director.

Detroit is predominantly Black, so joining a primarily White workplace at 20 years old was daunting. Many assumed they knew my background, but they didn't. The stress I faced at work was both external and internal.

I started my risk management and wellness career as a summer intern for the world's largest insurance brokerage firm. The firm's partnership with the Inroads program, which accelerates underrepresented talent, led me to this valuable opportunity. This experience deeply impacted my self-image, authenticity, and mindset.

Work was a world of juxtaposition - an incredible internship opportunity with exposure to a lucrative, technical, and creative career mixed with daily microaggressions and anxiety about everything from my complexion and style to my hair and dialect.

I experienced leaders who told me it was all a game I needed to play. Some leaders recognized my prowess for problem-solving, and others wouldn't even make eye contact or speak to me.

The complex web of daily experiences and emotions took its toll on my mindset and health. Even though I had graduated from a private university in Illinois and had studied abroad in Spain, there was a sense of permanence about work that let me know that I had arrived in the so-called "real world."

I loved risk management, though I always wanted to be a business leader. My natural propensity for analytics, data, and making practical sense of complex issues was a powerful asset. It was incredible to build skills in operational, financial, hazard, and strategic risk and learn the role insurance plays in our world.

Still, I contended daily with not feeling like I belonged in that environment. The feelings were so overwhelming, and I realized that it wasn't just coming from the outside; it was coming from inside of me.

I was afraid constantly. Afraid to fail, afraid to be judged, and afraid to be seen. Where did the fear come from? My own grandmother. The same woman who taught me that I was beautiful, smart, and worthy of all great things also taught me to fear White people. It triggered me. I was further impacted the day my boss told me, "Princess, you don't look like a risk manager."

Being told that I didn't look like something that I was working so hard to be was hard to swallow, but that moment became pivotal in my life, career, and holistic health.

Instead of accepting and ingesting my boss's quip, I asked her what she meant by it. Stunned by the question, she stammered the answer, "I meant nothing." A light bulb went off at that moment - she genuinely didn't know why, or at least she wasn't willing to own the reason.

Immediately, I took my power back from fear! She couldn't articulate the complex web of stories, stereotypes, and narratives that made her say that any more than I could express the depth of my triggers. From that point, I knew I would never let fear stop me from becoming whatever I wanted.

I transformed my mindset and skills to combat fear. Over the past two decades, I've built an incredible risk management, wellness, HR, and learning design career that prepared me for the work I do today - speaking globally, building an enterprise, and leading organizations that want to take their wellness, inclusion, and next-gen initiatives from awareness to action. Learn more at www.gobeyondwell.com.

Biography and Contact Information for Princess Castleberry

Princess Castleberry is a Professional Speaker, Wellness and Risk Management Consultant, and CEO at GO BEYOND WELL. She works with organizations that want to protect their people, purpose, and profits. She takes their wellness, inclusion, and leadership initiatives from awareness to action.

She has consulted across many industries, solving complex people and operations problems with over two decades of global risk, HR, and wellness expertise.

She commands the stage with a bold presence that lives up to her name, a thoughtful balance of humor, and actionable frameworks that position leaders from the C-Suite to the front line to take action.

Email: princess@gobeyondwell.com

Phone: 313-207-7366

Website: www.gobeyondwell.com

SUCCESS HONOR ROLL

Jason Roberts, CEO

Frontline Careers

After nearly 20 years of successfully climbing the career ladder, Jason realized something needed to give in his life. The stress of the corporate grind had finally taken its toll, and following a stroke at 42 years old, Jason knew he had to find greater purpose and meaning to his work.

Two years later, Jason left Corporate America to launch Frontline Careers, a workplace assessment company based in Southern California. Using their proprietary Frontline Friendly℠ workplace assessment, he and his team now help businesses across the country improve their bottom line by enhancing the employee experience of their frontline staff.

Over the years, Jason has coached many people to take advantage of learning opportunities on someone else's dime. Frontline Careers is his personal testimony of doing just that while finding better alignment with one's values and purpose.

Contact Information:

Website: https://frontlinecareers.com

Email: jason@frontlinecareers.com

CHAPTER THREE

HOW TO OVERCOME PROCRASTINATION

Procrastination is a saboteur of potential that can lead to negative consequences in your personal and professional lives. It can cause stress, feelings of guilt, inadequacy, and loss of confidence.

Procrastination can strain relationships and raise questions as to reliability and trust.

Over time, putting off tasks and obligations undermines opportunities for growth, promotion, and learning.

The habit of procrastination can result in poor mental health, increased anxiety, and a sense of dissatisfaction with your own life trajectory.

Victor Kiam said, ***"Procrastination is opportunity's assassin."***

Christopher Parker also said something interesting, ***"Procrastination is like a credit card. It's a lot of fun until you get thc bill."***

Overcoming procrastination is critical right now because many of us are at a point where we want to move forward, get things done, and make the rest of our lives more productive.

One way to determine if we will accomplish our goals or not is whether we permit procrastination in our lives.

What is Procrastination?

Procrastination is putting off until tomorrow what should have been done today. For some of us, it is putting off until tomorrow what should have been done last week.

Procrastination is abandoning the *now* for the *nothing.*

In other words, when we procrastinate, we are like the farmer who has a magnificent farm, fertile land, and seeds to plant but does nothing with them.

Many of us have dreams, things we want to be, do, and have - and a world of possibilities awaiting us. But we procrastinate instead of planting the seeds or doing something with those dreams.

Procrastination is a learned habit.

You don't wake up a procrastinator, nor are you born one. I've heard people say, *"I'm a born procrastinator."* No, you're not!

Procrastination is a learned habit. It is the thief of dreams and time. None of your goals or dreams will be realized if you procrastinate.

Procrastination is the most insidious obstacle to your success.

Procrastination is the thief of time and opportunity.

All of us are given the same amount of time: sixty seconds in a minute, sixty minutes in an hour, and twenty-four hours in a day. We all have the same amount of time, but what we do with that time determines the quality of our lives.

An important scriptural principle provides, *"To all things, there's a season."*

Thus, every opportunity has a season. It passes on to someone else if you do not act on an opportunity. Many of us have had opportunities that we did not act upon, and we paid the price.

Procrastination is the thief of life.

I was recently at a funeral, and I looked at the tombstones and wondered *how many people were buried with their dreams. How many people in those graves had procrastinated about achieving their greatness?*

Procrastination is the thief of all that is good for you. It can keep you from living your purpose and realizing your destiny.

Procrastination flies on the wings of excuses.

Many of us are procrastinators but don't want to admit it. We make excellent, plausible excuses for not achieving the things we desire. The better the excuse, the worse it is.

CHARACTERISTICS OF A PROCRASTINATOR

Most people do not acknowledge being a procrastinator. However, when we examine the characteristics of a procrastinator, we often find a little procrastination in ourselves.

Once we acknowledge that we have

procrastinator traits, we can begin the process of eliminating this negative habit.

1. **The first characteristic of a procrastinator is being afraid to fail.**

Many of us are like that. We're afraid to fail. Opportunities often present themselves in our lives, and we say, *"I'd love to do it, but I'm afraid to fail."* We avoid tasks because of a fear of not meeting expectations.

2. **The second characteristic of a procrastinator is believing that you cannot do it.**

Henry Ford said, *"If you believe you can or believe you can't, you're right."*

If you find it hard to believe you can do something, you may be a procrastinator.

3. **The third characteristic of a procrastinator is not knowing where to start.**

They say, *"I don't know where to start."*

Many of us are guilty of this characteristic. We have had important goals or grand visions and dreams but needed help figuring out where to start.

If those words have ever come out, you may

be a procrastinator.

4. **The fourth signal of a procrastinator is waiting for the right time.**

They say, *"I'm just waiting for the right time to start."*

Many people in sales or network marketing can identify with this characteristic. Imagine being at the end of the month with only two days left, and you're waiting for the right time to take action.

You make statements like, *"There are only two days left. I will tidy up my desk so I can prepare for next month. Then I'm going to start next month with a bang."*

Guess what! Next month and the month after that, you do the same thing. I call them the "*I'm going to*" people. *I'm going to do this or get that.* They will always have things they never get around to doing.

5. **The fifth sign of a procrastinator is focusing on immediate rather than long-term benefits.**

They spend dollar time on penny jobs. One of the illusions of procrastination is being busy. Every activity takes time and energy, but not every action is equally important in achieving your goals.

If you focus on performing penny jobs instead of dollar activities, you may be a procrastinator.

6. **The sixth characteristic of a procrastinator is the pursuit of perfection.**

You wait for everything to be perfect before you get started.

A friend used to say, *"I've got to get my ducks in a row."*

That was another way of saying I've got to wait for everything to be perfect before I start. Does anyone really care if your ducks are in a row?

7. **The seventh characteristic of a procrastinator is waiting for someone to help.**

Many people live their lives waiting for someone to help them achieve their goals. That *"someone else"* may be waiting on you. You are waiting on them, and they are waiting on you, which makes both of you procrastinators.

If we observe any of these characteristics in

ourselves, this is a clue we need to get to work and address it.

Another characteristic of a procrastinator that is associated with waiting for someone else's help is letting other people interrupt your flow.

This is not to say that you should not help others or make yourself available to people in need. But evaluate each situation on a case-by-case basis and critically examine why they need help and if there is a pattern.

When people interrupt your flow with their crisis, be sympathetic and attentive.

Respond in a way that feels right. However, suppose the same person has the same or similar crisis repeatedly. In that case, it may indicate a deeper issue that has little to do with you.

Do not become so involved with helping other people with their issues or endeavors that you lose sight of your own goals. My dad used to say, *"I spent so much time drinking to my brother's health that I ruined my own."*

WHY DO PEOPLE PROCRASTINATE?

If procrastination can have such a negative impact on life, why do people procrastinate?

1. **Fear of failure.** Thomas Edison said, *"I failed my way to success."* Failure is not a bad thing. It can be a dress rehearsal for success.

Theodore Roosevelt said something very profound:

"It's hard to fail, but it's worse never to have tried to succeed."

If we don't try, we can't fail. The fear of failure can paralyze us, so we never accomplish our goals.

2. **Focus on the negative.** The first words we learn as a child are *no, stop*, and *don't.* Once we start talking, we learn the words *shut up.* Based on our childhood, we can be so consumed by *no, stop, and don't* that these words become our frame of reference.

Instead of saying, *"I can do this,"* They focus on, *I can't do this.* This is not possible.

Some people look for all the reasons

something won't work. If we are raised in an environment of criticism, we can spend so much time focusing on why things won't work that we never do what we can to get what we want.

3. **Lack of worthiness.** We may procrastinate pursuing our goals if we don't feel worthy.

Everything in life is processed through the lenses of our self-image and self-esteem. These qualities are like glasses. We see everything through the lenses of those glasses.

If we have low self-image, we may feel unworthy of our goals. We may be competent, and yet we don't go for it.

I've seen people in a corporate environment who are excellent employees. They understand their job and get things done.

Yet, when they are given an opportunity for promotion to a management position, they say no, *"I don't want to manage people. I don't want to be responsible for others."*. They've been doing the job all along, but suddenly, they feel unworthy.

Feelings of unworthiness can cause procrastination.

4. **Addiction to perfection.** A fourth cause of procrastination is an addiction to perfection.

"Don't let addiction to perfection keep you from enjoying the ecstasy of completion."

Being addicted to perfection may sound like a good thing, but that same addiction can keep you from taking action.

We already have everything we need to get everything we desire. Addiction to perfection can undermine our gratitude for the blessings we already possess.

We have defined procrastination, examined its characteristics, and examined how and why we do it.

Let us now examine how to overcome procrastination.

TWELVE KEYS TO OVERCOME PROCRASTINATION

1. **Realize that procrastination is a state of mind—a learned habit.**

No one is born a procrastinator; it is

something that we learn either actively or passively.

Since procrastination is a state of mind and a learned habit, we can change and overcome it.

The second law of success provides:

"Be not conformed to this world, but be transformed by renewing your mind."

If you are a procrastinator, you don't have to stay there. The renewing of your mind can transform you. You can think new thoughts and learn new habits.

We often learn procrastination as children. As parents, we know we can say one thing, but our children will learn by watching what we do. If we are procrastinators, our children will see us as indecisive and unable to move forward on projects or plans. Observing our parents is often our first lesson in becoming a procrastinator.

2. **Recognize that procrastination is the leading cause of failure.**

More people fail by not trying than by getting into the game and taking the blows and bruises.

Procrastination is expensive. Think of the

opportunities you missed, the jobs you didn't take, and the relationships you could have had. Revisit the good things that could have happened in your life but didn't because you procrastinated.

One of the worst things about procrastination is that the more you procrastinate, the worse it gets. Procrastination is like cancer. Untreated, it will consume and kill your body.

It is like a mortgage. You missed one month even though you had the money, but instead decided, *"I'm going to take a vacation and take care of the mortgage when I return."* Then you miss the second month. You tell yourself, *"I've been here before, I've missed months before, they'll work with me, and I'll catch up by paying for two months."*

In the third month, you send one payment, and the bank sends it back, notifying you that you need to pay all three months and a penalty immediately to bring your mortgage up to date.

Procrastination is expensive because the more you do it, the more costly and devastating it becomes. It is like the farmer who has the seed and field but never plants his corn. He and his family will not eat corn, no matter how hungry they are.

3. Stick to a definite schedule.

Without a schedule, you will not be successful. Tony Robbins says, *"Anything you don't schedule will not get done."*

A schedule gives you a framework and a blueprint for each day.

Can you imagine building a skyscraper without following a blueprint? Living a life without a schedule is like building a skyscraper without a blueprint. How it's going to turn out is unpredictable.

4. Always be on time.

Being on time and having a definite schedule go hand in hand. But if you don't stick to it, it's worthless.

A student commented on how impressed he was that I have been doing my success mentorship class every Saturday morning at eight o'clock for years. I told him that showing up every Saturday morning was my therapy. It helps to validate my schedule.

When you commit to always be on time, it keeps you going and gives you a frame of reference to say, *"I can do this! And I always do everything on time."*

When I attended my first Tony Robbins seminar, I had no intention of walking on hot coals. By the end of the session, I walked on 16 feet of burning coals and paid to do it.

I realized it was about overcoming my fear of fire and demonstrating that I could do something I thought impossible. Once I had walked on the coals, I had a different frame of reference.

5. Operate from a prioritized daily list.

One of the pitfalls to overcoming procrastination is making lists that are not prioritized. It is very easy to spend dollar time on penny jobs.

When you work from a prioritized list, you have already given your mental energy to establish the importance and value of each task you will perform each day. That value is determined based on your goals, vision, and purpose.

Ask yourself,

"What is the best use of my time right now, considering my goals, vision, and purpose?"

Working from a prioritized list means that you have a series of things to do that are organized in their level of importance to achieving your goals.

6. **Make a realistic assessment of the time required to achieve each activity on your to-do list.**

There are pitfalls to avoid. You can make your list but need a realistic assessment of how much time each activity may take. There may be an activity that takes two hours, but you have allocated only fifteen minutes on your list.

Guess what? The activity will not be done, and you will probably be frustrated.

Don't simply make a list without a realistic assessment of the time it takes to complete each activity. Allow sufficient time for planning, preparation, and execution of each activity/task on your to-do list.

PRESIDENT ABRAHAM LINCOLN SAID,

"GIVE ME SIX HOURS TO CHOP DOWN A TREE, AND I WILL SPEND THE FIRST FOUR SHARPENING THE AXE."

Preparation is sharpening your axe – your skill set - to accomplish your scheduled activities most effectively.

7. **Plan to work on one activity at a time until it is completed.**

I am not a believer in multitasking. I prefer doing one activity/task at a time.

My definition of multitasking is doing individual tasks at different times.

Set up your schedule of activities to allow you to do one task while another is taking place. As you prioritize your tasks, organize them so they can be done sequentially and simultaneously.

For example, your task may be to bake a cake. Once you've mixed the batter and placed the cake in the oven – with thirty-five minutes to bake, you can perform another task during that time. But if you attempt to mix the cake batter and iron clothes simultaneously, something will probably get burned.

8. Analyze goals or activities and break them down into doable chunks.

Completing one activity/task at a time creates a cycle that helps build your confidence.

When we are confronted with big, complex goals, there may be a tendency to procrastinate. To avoid this tendency, analyze the goal and break it down into doable chunks.

For example, if your daughter is a high school student who wants to attend Harvard University. That's a big goal.

Consider starting by analyzing and breaking this lofty goal down into chunks. First, your daughter must graduate from high school with close to a 4.0 average. While in high school, she must get information about the procedure to submit her application to Harvard.

She will have to assemble financial aid information and complete the necessary documentation. It will be essential to schedule necessary testing information or college board examinations. Your daughter should also contact and develop a relationship with the Harvard admissions department.

When you have a big complex goal, break it down into smaller segments or steps that can be handled until completion.

How do you eat an elephant? One bite at a time. To quote a Chinese proverb,

"*The journey of a thousand miles begins with a single step.*"

9. Hold yourself accountable.

If you task yourself with achieving a particular goal, at the end of the day, you are responsible for achieving it. Accountability requires constantly monitoring your progress and taking responsibility for the results you create.

Without accountability, there are no guardrails to keep you on track to your success.

Your accountability mantra should be, *"If it's to be, it's up to me."*

Be patient with yourself. You did not become a procrastinator overnight and will not overcome procrastination overnight. Procrastination is a learned skill. It takes time to unlearn it—small, consistent steps over time lead to significant, remarkable success.

10. Start small.

It requires a complete change in your mindset and actions to stop procrastinating. Once you decide to stop procrastinating, start small and take time to honor yourself for the little victories.

A primary goal could be getting up every day at the same time. As you accomplish that goal, you may find that you're waking at the same time every day but feel tired when you wake up. Your next goal may be to go to bed earlier each night.

Starting small lets you celebrate your little victories, get excited about your accomplishments, and make necessary adjustments. This gradual approach allows you to monitor and assess the actual time needed to complete a particular task. This functional assessment can help you avoid setting yourself up for failure.

Rather than attempting to do ten tasks and accomplishing only three, adjust your task selection and activity level to get better results. For example, set a goal for five tasks and work towards achieving all of them.

Once you have successfully accomplished the five tasks, you can extend your to-do list to six, then to seven, and finally accomplish all ten tasks.

11. Get help.

Being a procrastinator is like any other kind of addiction. No matter how hard you try to overcome procrastination by yourself, you seem to fall back into the habit.

As with any person with an addiction, you need help. It is extremely difficult to overcome procrastination at the same level of consciousness that created it. Outside assistance is often necessary.

You may need to take a course in time management or in getting organized if you regularly waste time looking for things. Set aside your ego. Be honest with yourself and acknowledge that you have a problem.

Getting help can also create a mastermind vibration where two or more are gathered on one accord, producing more power and ability to get things done.

12. Keep going and growing.

Overcoming procrastination is an evolutionary process. You didn't get there overnight and won't solve it overnight. But if you are committed to keep going and growing, you will evolve into a *"Do it now"* person capable of being, doing, and having anything you desire.

CHAPTER SUMMARY

Procrastination is putting off until tomorrow what should have been done yesterday or last week.

Procrastination is a learned habit.

Procrastinators are afraid to fail, believe they cannot do it, don't know where to start, wait for the right time, focus on immediate rather than long-term benefits, pursue perfection, and wait for someone else to help.

People procrastinate because of fear of failure, focusing on the negative, lack of worthiness, and addiction to perfection.

Twelve keys to Overcome Procrastination

1. Realize that procrastination is a state of mind and a learned habit.
2. Realize that procrastination is the leading cause of failure.
3. Create and stick to a definite schedule.
4. Commit to always being on time.
5. Work from a prioritized list.

6. Make a realistic assessment of the time required to complete each activity and the preparation required.
7. Plan to handle one activity at a time until each is done.
8. Analyze complex goals and activities and break them down into doable chunks.
9. Hold yourself accountable, but be patient with your growth.
10. Start small, grow your confidence, skills, and ability to get things done, and do them.
11. Get help from someone who's been where you are and has transformed how you want to be changed. Use the power of the mastermind.
12. Keep going and growing. The only time you ever have is now.

Yesterday is a canceled check and tomorrow is a promissory note. We are living our lives now. When you assess the best use of your time each moment, consider your goals, vision, and purpose, and act accordingly, nothing is impossible.

Many of us struggle with procrastination at some point in our lives. These twelve keys to overcome procrastination can transform your life.

Using these keys, you can be what you want to be, do what you want to do, and have whatever you want to have, always knowing that the *best is yet to come.*

GREATEST VICTORY CONTRIBUTOR, THE REV. BERNETTE L. JONES

Background

I'm a Universal Foundation For Better Living (UFBL) ordained minister, spiritual teacher, and board member of UFBL and the Johnnie Colemon Theological Seminary (JCTS). I am the senior minister at the One God, One Thought Center for Better Living in Baltimore, MD, a New Thought Christian church and affiliate church of UFBL.

I am a native of Baltimore, Maryland and a resident for all seventy-two years of my life.

My parents migrated from Scotland Neck, a little town in North Carolina, and settled in Baltimore in the early fifties. I was born in 1951, the third of seven children.

I attended Towson University for my undergraduate degree. We grew up spending what seemed like all our days and nights attending a little Baptist church around the corner from us.

However, I felt like something was missing at about eight years old. I can recall thinking that they made it seem like if you weren't in that little church, you weren't going to heaven. This did not sit well with me. So, I wanted nothing else to do with church and decided I wouldn't go if I didn't have to.

My Path to Ministry

On entering college, I said to God, "I'm not going back to church. If there's anything you want me to know, you will have to tell me directly." And that's precisely what happened.

My spiritual journey started by studying ancient wisdom traditions and universal religions in philosophy at Towson University. Then, I discovered there was more to religion and spirituality than what was taught in that little Baptist church.

I knew that I was called to ministry, but I was running away from it.

I went into business. When it failed, I went to the Baltimore Urban League and became Vice

President for nine years.

I prayed for guidance, and God gave me the idea of designing my life by building *"a pyramid in my consciousness"* and then expressing it to others.

I surrendered and became a founding member of the One God One Thought Center for Better Living. I had planned on only staying for six months, but this year, I have been there for twenty-nine years and Senior Minister for twenty years.

My first mentor, Wendell Phillips, a United Church of Christ minister, said to me, *"Ministry doesn't have to look any particular way. It can look however God communicates it to you"*. He was real and alive, and I saw a path to ministry where I could truly express God as Spirit guided me.

The Holy Spirit guided me to the Johnnie Colemon Theological Seminary. Before I was even ordained, I got a call asking me if I would be the Senior Minister at the church in Baltimore. I found my life's work there and have loved every minute of the twenty years I have been the spiritual leader.

Life Lessons & Overcoming Obstacles

My first major failure was in business. This led me to ministry because God was my only source of mental and spiritual solace. Along with my partners, we acquired a distributorship for beauty products. We had thirty workers, six stores, and sales of $1.2 million in the first year.

After four years, it collapsed. My heart was broken after my relationship with a Kenyan guy who was my business partner and who I believed I would marry ended.

I remember screaming, *"God, oh God, help me!"* Then I clearly heard the response, *"I was wondering when you were going to ask. You thought you could do it by yourself."*

That was a pivotal point and a powerful lesson for me.

I was angry, but I later appreciated the role my spiritual foundation played in my development. God showed me the Conscious Life Design system. This spiritual maintenance support system enabled me to structure my life to become an enjoyable journey. I have a joyful life now.

Those first years in ministry were challenging. Early in my ministry, I had to be hospitalized, and board members made decisions without my knowledge. In another situation, someone told a lie on me. Though I felt betrayed, I had to forgive and grow spiritually when I realized that the consciousness of some people in the congregation had not yet evolved.

I never aspired to be a minister. But I was willing and open.

When I became the organization's full-time pastor, minister, and CEO, it wasn't an egotistical journey at all. People would ask, *"What is it like being a black female minister?"*

I never saw myself as a black female minister. I only saw myself as God's instrument. It was not easy, but I've overcome the negative self-image and self-talk. I learned to be spirit-led by meditating and praying for hours until I developed intimacy with the spirit. It was the best thing that ever happened to me.

Dealing with Distractions

There will always be distractions. Many times, they're so subtle they go unnoticed. Television used to distract me from studying and spending time in solitude. Some distractions seem good, but you must decide what's more important. When I learned to meditate, I quit cigarettes cold turkey because my soul's growth was more important, and it felt better being able to breathe.

My Passion and Greatest Victory

Being a minister allows me to witness people discovering who they really are and their greatness. Leadership cannot be ego-driven. It's an inspired vision of the highest and best for the people. Being a good leader requires leading with integrity, excellence, and stamina. Integrity is simply being honest and transparent, while excellence is giving the highest quality service with what you have to work with. Stamina is about staying the course and having the endurance to continue.

Spirit-driven leadership spans the broader spectrum of having one mind, the mind of Christ. Much of my work is helping people see each other's leadership ability; that way, when I toss the ball to them, they'll know what to do with it. It equips and empowers them to do something they never thought they could do. It is a mastermind consciousness. No one does ministry alone: that's why I say it's not my church. It's God's church.

I'm going to write a book titled *"The Eclectic Ecclesia "* based on empowering uniquely gifted people using Truth principles. I'm constantly seeking committed people sent by God to address the community and global issues.

My greatest victory has been overcoming my fear of failure. I ran from ministry for many years because I didn't think it would be fulfilling. I was afraid of being a Senior Minister and Pastor. However, something is compelling about the call to loving service and being the answer to somebody's prayer. It's been the most satisfying and fulfilling thing I've ever done.

How did the Twelve Universal Laws of Success book come to your attention, and do you prefer any particular chapter?

Dr. John Chissell, a noted Baltimore physician, had a signed copy of Dr. Harris' book. It had an inscription that read, *"Continued success with your important work. God bless you "*.

This was in 1998, just a year after it was published. I had given away my original copy and planned to buy another one. Then I remembered Dr. Chissell's daughters donated his entire library to the One God One Thought Center when he transitioned. I was at the church, and I said, *"Spirit, I know that book is in here; lead me to it."* It led me right to the book.

This book is a little handbook that everyone should have. It is well-structured, and I learned to do my ministerial study using the technique you referred to in the introduction. Each law is broken down so you can work on it individually to build your success muscle.

What would you say if you could talk to your younger self 25, 35, or 40 years ago?

I would say, "You don't know everything, yet the Real you knows everything. Find someone who has navigated the past successfully and learn from them. You don't have to reinvent the wheel, nor do you have to do everything in one day.

Learn from others and improve on what you've learned". I had to tell myself that mentorship is good and that good people have trod the path before me. *"You're not the first or the only one, and you're not going to be the last one. So don't try to do it yourself."*

If I had to do it all again, I would avoid dwelling on whether I could have been much further on my success journey. I'm content knowing that I'm exactly where I'm meant to be, doing exactly what I'm supposed to do. I've heard Dr. Johnnie Colemon and many other leaders say, "The best is yet to come." The journey isn't over as long as you're here and still moving.

What would you tell your future self?

You've left a great legacy and foundation for others to build the next leg of the journey. You've taught people the wisdom of loving God, loving oneself, and loving others. When people hear your name, they will be inspired to build something powerful and amazing that serves others".

What message would you give to people seeking success in their lives?

Attaining a higher consciousness of living is possible. But you must reach beyond your limitations. Even at seventy-two years old, there are some great things I'm still ready to do.

It's all about perspective. Raise your level of consciousness and live from there. Examine what you've been saying to yourself and choose whether you want to say something different that will lead you somewhere different.

Biography and Contact Information

The Reverend Bernette Lee Jones has been the Senior Minister at the One God One Thought Center for Better Living in Baltimore, Maryland for over 20 years.

She has a bachelor's degree in business administration from Towson State University in Maryland and received ordination through The Universal Foundation for Better Living, Johnnie Colemon Theological Seminary in 2003.

Rev. Bernette is an author whose work is featured along with noted contemporary New Thought writers The Reverend Dr. Barbara King, Deepak Chopra, and Dr. Wayne Dyer in the book *"Wake Up: Live the Life You Love In Spirit."*

Since 1990, Reverend Bernette has been exploring and developing *"The LifeShop: Conscious Living System"* - a program for conscious living and personal transformation.

She currently serves as a board member of the

Universal Foundation for Better Living and as board chair for the Johnnie Colemon Theological Seminary.

In 2012, she received The Universal Foundation for Better Living Johnnie Colemon Award for Leadership Excellence.

Reverend Bernette Jones has one daughter, Kameel Hall, and one grandson, Ryan Lee Hall.

Rev. Bernette Lee Jones, Senior Minister, One God One Thought Center for Better Living, Inc.

Email: senior_minister@ogot.org

Founder, Consciousness Agency

Website: www.consciousnessagency.com

GREATEST VICTORY CONTRIBUTOR TROY WHITEHURST

Background

I grew up in Norfolk, Virginia, and initially pursued a college education in radio, television, and film. I have been involved in sports, teaching, and coaching basketball, as well as various leadership roles. Growing up in Virginia wasn't the best environment, but I knew I couldn't change it. I left intending to develop myself and then return to make a positive impact later.

Moving to a new city was a scary experience, but I needed to get out of my comfort zone, and moving allowed me to do that.

I initially thought of moving to Hollywood to pursue film and radio work. But I moved to Charlotte, North Carolina instead and decided to follow Christ.

Life Lessons and Overcoming Obstacles One of my biggest challenges was writing my book and dealing with an unexpected illness. Two months after I got my dream job, being a basketball coach, I started losing feeling in the left side of my body. I got nervous after it began on the right side and went to a specialist. She diagnosed me with multiple sclerosis.

I thought my life was over. I did some research, changed my diet, and started utilizing natural supplements. I had to renew my mind about food and activate my faith by praying healing scriptures over my body. My mindset became, *"Nothing tastes as good as being healthy feels."*

After eighteen months, my symptoms reversed, and I was able to get back to an everyday, active life. However, I couldn't resume my previous activities, so I started working in insurance. It has helped me generate income and gave me the freedom and flexibility I needed to focus on my health.

What is your greatest passion and victory?

I've just completed writing my first book entitled, *"Choose to Be Happy."* I chose that title because happiness is a choice, and everyone is responsible for their own happiness. We all have gates of awareness that lead to our souls. Our eyes, ears, nose, and mouth are entranceways for information.

In my book, I talk about guarding those gates. If we are not guarding our gates and examining what enters our souls, we can be programmed by them. God had to deprogram me from my life in media. My greatest victory is knowing that I can't do anything without God.

How did The Twelve Universal Laws of Success book come to your attention, and do you prefer any particular chapter?

My journey took a significant turn when I discovered *The Twelve Universal Laws of Success.* It was the first book I read while I was on campus. Reading it and connecting with Dr. Harris positively transformed my life.

It is a very inspiring book. I appreciate its biblical nature and that it is based on principles and universal laws.

The most powerful chapter for me is the introduction, which describes the types of people in life: the wonderers, the wanderers, the spectators, and the players. As an athlete, I didn't want to be outside the stadium just wandering and not knowing what was happening. I wanted to be on the field of play.

What message would you give to people seeking success in their lives?

My message of success is that we serve a God of the impossible. My situation taught me that there will always be unexpected challenges or situations.

The question is, what do you do when faced with these situations? Do you give up, or do you activate your faith? When your faith is activated, fear disappears. They cannot coexist.

Always believe in the possibilities of what God can do. Learn to pivot, not toward drugs, alcohol, or bad relationships, but toward where God is pointing and leading you.

Biography and Contact Information for Troy Whitehurst

Troy Whitehurst is a native of Norfolk, Virginia. He is currently the managing agent for the TW Insurance Service LLC.

Troy has worn many hats in his lifetime,

including filmmaker, radio host, and coach. A North Carolina A&T State University graduate, he majored in Marketing and Entrepreneurship.

Troy Whitehurst is the author of *"Choose To Be Happy"* Joy Comes from the Lord.

Troy Whitehurst

TW Insurance LLC

Life Health Worksite Benefits

704-819-2299

Websites: www.wegetyoucovered.com

www.troywhitehurst.com

SUCCESS HONOR ROLL

Brother Minister Zumbi X. Shawala (Chris Johnson)

Brother Minister Zumbi X. Shawala (Chris Johnson) is the founder of Liberty Hall Media Group and the author of **G.O.A.T. (GOSPEL OF AFRONOMICS THEOLOGY).**

Brother Minister has built a following through an online radio show called **FROM MIND 2 MARKET** (2007-2012) on LIBRadio **(www.LIBRadio.com)** and serves as a board member of the Nat Turner Library Foundation in Virginia.

As a business and financial thought leader, Brother Minister's economic philosophy is for people to be taught the proper tools, value systems, and mindset to overcome their financial challenges.

He also addresses the economic challenges of the hip-hop and African World Communities. He believes these communities have the right to fulfill their economic destinies through microenterprise, entrepreneurship, and *"community angel investing."*

Contact Information

Liberty Hall Media Group

240 State St #2452

Albany, NY 12220

518.512.9972

Libertyhallpress@gmail.com

www.amazon.com/dp/1626765553

ACHIEVERS INTERVIEWED ON THE SUCCESS TALK PODCAST

Over the last year and a half, I have interviewed 100+ achievers from all walks of life.

The life stories of these very special people were an inspiration to complete this book.

K'emo A'akhutera
Jonathan Beatty (Chief Bookman)
Anthony Bodie, Jr.
Dr. Rubye Braye
Jinger Callwood
Princess Castleberry
Karen Creecy
Chris Corinthian
Oscar Joe Dais
Jimmy Davis
Hikia Dixon
Pamela Ellis
Patrick Freeman
Dr. James Graham
Tia Hamilton
Steve Hutchinson
Sunniej Jackson
Chris Johnson
Gievanty Jones
Jes Landau
Christi Love
Frank Marshall
Sheila Agnew McCoy
Faith Moore McKinney
Vee Mindful
Lemetrius Nolan
Jason Roberts
Coach David Smile
Linda Tate
Sheree Victorian
Abundantly Wealthy Stan White
Attorney Wende Williams
Will Zanders
William Adams
Attorney Olivia S. Benson
Iva Brito
Bryce Britton
Dr. Erika Carter
Inga Faison Cavitt
Clarence Goggins
Kenya Crooks
William Daniels (I Am)
Reggie Davis
Kyle Dixon
Darrell Evans
Terry Gibson
Dr. Pamela Gurley
Mary Harris
Queen Mother Imakhu
Tyree Jennings
Rev. Bernette Jones
Randy Kates
Shermaine Lopez
Dawn Lovell
Stan Matthews
George McDaniel
Luvenia Graham Meekins
Quentin Moses
Dr. Jarret Patton
Roland & Dorensa Roberts
Will (Willie) Smith
Herman Taylor
Lorene Brown Watkins
Toni Melvin Whitaker
Dr. Craig Wright
Dr. John Artis
DeVonte Bennet Bey
Ken Brown
William Burton
Veronica Carter
Jay Clark
Mayah Collins
Shelly Currie
Hezekiah Davis
Tonya Debnam
Rory Douglas
Kalvin Evans
Stephanie Gore
Manny Hall
Cassandra Henderson
Janine Ingram
Danielle Paige Jeter
Gary Jones
Thomas C. Knox
Charlotte C. Louis
Sir Markadoo
Deidra Mayberry
Carrie McIntyre
Steve Miller
DeJohnna Owens
Derek Phillips
Madelyn Clark Robinson
Garry Spriggs
Seko Varner
Rexford White
Troy Whitehurst
Ricky Young

ABOUT THE AUTHOR

Dr. *Herbert Harris,* a graduate of Columbia University in New York City, is a retired attorney who has written numerous books including ***How To Make Money In Music***, a highly popular guide book to the music industry, ***The Twelve Universal Laws of Success*** a best-selling personal development book, and ***Solving The Race Issue In America***. His books have been translated into Chinese, French, Italian, Portuguese, Romanian, and Spanish.

Herbert is a former director of the ***Science of Living Institute*** under Dr. Frederick J. Eikerenkkotter, better known as "Rev. Ike". He is CEO of the LifeSkill Institute, Inc., an international personal and leadership development corporation.

Dr. Harris has spoken and done numerous seminars and workshops at churches, universities, and corporations throughout the country, including: the Ethical Culture Society, Unity Church, Ohio State University, Columbia University, Lucent Technology, and other businesses and organizations.

Presently Dr. Herbert Harris maintains a strong internet presence with the Success Mentorship Network and a busy speaking schedule at numerous churches, corporations, and organizations. He is an Elite Trainer with the LifeVantage Corporation, a publicly traded health and wellness company. Herbert is a ***"Million Dollar Earner"*** in the network marketing industry. Dr. Harris resides in North Carolina.

Agent: John Hughes 910-262-2680
Toll Free Phone: 800-570-4009
Email: herbert@herbertharris.com
Website: www.herbertharris.com
www.lifeskillinstitute.org

Contact: John Hughes 910-262-2680
www.herbertharris.com
herbert@herbertharris.com

Contact Information for Dr. Herbert Harris

Made in United States
Troutdale, OR
11/03/2026

56844655R00080